HOUSE C

CW00524008

European Union Committee

18th Report of Session 2007–08

The 2009 EC Budget

Report with Evidence

Ordered to be printed 8 July 2008 and published 15 July 2008

Published by the Authority of the House of Lords

London : The Stationery Office Limited
£11.00

HL Paper 140

The European Union Committee

The European Union Committee is appointed by the House of Lords "to consider European Union documents and other matters relating to the European Union". The Committee has seven Sub-Committees which are:

Economic and Financial Affairs, and International Trade (Sub-Committee A)
Internal Market (Sub-Committee B)
Foreign Affairs, Defence and Development Policy (Sub-Committee C)
Environment and Agriculture (Sub-Committee D)
Law and Institutions (Sub-Committee E)
Home Affairs (Sub-Committee F)
Social and Consumer Affairs (Sub-Committee G)

Our Membership

The Members of the European Union Committee are:

Lord Grenfell (Chairman)
Lord Blackwell
Baroness Cohen of Pimlico
Lord Dykes
Lord Freeman
Lord Harrison
Baroness Howarth of Breckland
Lord Jopling
Lord Kerr of Kinlochard
Lord Maclennan of Rogart

Lord Mance
Lord Plumb
Lord Powell of Bayswater
Lord Roper
Lord Sewel
Baroness Symons of Vernham Dean
Lord Tomlinson
Lord Wade
Lord Wright of Richmond

The Members of the Sub-Committee which carried out this inquiry (Economic and Financial Affairs, and International Trade, Sub-Committee A) are:

Baroness Cohen of Pimlico (Chairman)
Lord Haskins
Lord Kerr of Kinlochard
Lord Maclennan of Rogart
Lord Moser

Lord Moser
Lord Renton of Steinberg
Lord Steinberg
Lord Trimble
Lord Watson of Richmond

Information about the Committee

The reports and evidence of the Committee are published by and available from The Stationery Office. For information freely available on the web, our homepage is:

http://www.parliament.uk/parliamentary_committees/lords_eu_select_committee.cfm

There you will find many of our publications, along with press notices, details of membership and forthcoming meetings, and other information about the ongoing work of the Committee and its Sub-Committees, each of which has its own homepage.

General Information

General information about the House of Lords and its Committees, including guidance to witnesses, details of current inquiries and forthcoming meetings is on the internet at
http://www.parliament.uk/about_lords/about_lords.cfm

Contacts for the European Union Committee

Contact details for individual Sub-Committees are given on the website.

General correspondence should be addressed to the Clerk of the European Union Committee, Committee Office, House of Lords, London, SW1A OPW
The telephone number for general enquiries is 020 7219 5791.
The Committee's email address is euclords@parliament.uk

CONTENTS

Oral Evidence

Ms Kitty Ussher MP, Economic Secretary, Mr Jean-Christophe Gray, Team Leader, Head of EU Finances, Mr Paul Bunsell, EC Annual Budget, HM Treasury

NOTE: References in the text of the report are as follows:
(Q) refers to a question in oral evidence
(p) refers to a page of written evidence

FOREWORD—What this report is about

This report informs the House about the Commission's proposals for the 2009 General Budget of the European Communities. The report summarises the significant proposed changes to funding under each of the budget headings. We have been aided in this by oral evidence from the Economic Secretary to HM Treasury (Kitty Ussher MP) and a written Explanatory Memorandum from HM Treasury.

This is the third budget to be drawn up under the current Financial Perspective, the agreement which sets spending ceilings over a seven year period. The multi-annual framework is well established and consequently this is an unexceptional budget. However, we share the Government's concerns that appropriations should be set at a level that matches amounts that can be realistically spent under each budget Heading. We also note that the margin—the difference between proposed spending levels and the maximum permitted under the Financial Perspective—may not be large enough to cover unforeseen expenditure under Headings 3 (Citizenship, Freedom, Security and Justice) and 4 (The EU as a Global Partner).

While looking specifically at the 2009 Preliminary Draft Budget, we have also briefly considered the review of the budget which the Commission has commenced, ahead of the negotiations on the next Financial Perspective. The public consultation period has just finished, and we look forward to the publication of detailed proposals by the Commission. The Committee's response to the consultation, submitted earlier this year, is printed at Appendix 2.

We also note that the budget does not demonstrate clearly the amounts that it is proposed be spent on items that cut across the budget headings, and we support the Government's suggestion that more could be done to highlight funding on topics that are distributed across the budget.

The 2009 EC Budget

CHAPTER 1: INTRODUCTION

1. This is the fifth consecutive year that we have scrutinised the EC Budget on the basis of oral evidence from the Government before the First Reading of the Preliminary Budget in the Council. The Committee decided in the last Parliament that taking evidence from the Government at such an early stage in the budgetary process was the most effective way in which we could fulfil our parliamentary obligation to scrutinise proposed EU legislation and ensure greater accountability and transparency.[1]

2. This year we received an Explanatory Memorandum on the Provisional Draft Budget from HM Treasury dated 2 June; on the basis of this document we took oral evidence from the Economic Secretary to the Treasury, Kitty Ussher MP, on 11 June. Both the Explanatory Memorandum and the transcript of oral evidence are printed with this report.

3. Although for the most part the annual EC Budget is determined by policies previously agreed as part of the Financial Perspective, scrutiny of the annual EC Budget remains an important means of making the process more transparent. The aim of the Committee's reports on the EC Budget is to inform the House of issues relating to the Budget and to scrutinise the Government's position before the Commission's Preliminary Draft Budget is considered at the Budget Council which takes place this year on 17 July. Scrutiny of the Government's position is particularly important given that the UK is a net contributor to the EC budget, and we appreciate the Government's effort to assist us in our scrutiny.

4. This report is the European Union Select Committee's main contribution to the scrutiny of the EC Budget. However, as part of our regular scrutiny role, we will continue to consider the Budget until it is adopted. We will also consider any Preliminary Draft Amending Budget presented by the Commission.

5. Appendix 3 contains a brief guide to the annual European budget procedure and there is a glossary at Appendix 4. We make this report to the House for information.

---

[1] European Union Committee, 1st Report (2002–03): *Review of Scrutiny of European Legislation* (HL 15).

CHAPTER 2: THE 2009 PRELIMINARY DRAFT BUDGET

Individual Spending Programmes and the Financial Perspective

6.   Spending in the annual EC Budget is currently divided into eight categories:

      (a) Competitiveness for Growth and Employment;

      (b) Cohesion for Growth and Employment;

      (c) Preservation and Management of Natural Resources;

      (d) Freedom, Security and Justice;

      (e) Citizenship;

      (f) The EU as a Global Partner;

      (g) Administration; and

      (h) Compensation.

7.   These categories are pre-determined by the multi-annual Financial Perspective agreement between the European Council, the Commission and the European Parliament. This agreement provides the financial framework for the EC over a period of seven years, and sets both a ceiling for total EC expenditure, defined in terms of a percentage of EU Gross National Income (GNI), and annual ceilings for each of the expenditure categories. The 2009 Budget is the third to be proposed under the current Financial Perspective, which governs Budgets from 2007 to 2013.

8.   As in every year, the 2009 Preliminary Draft Budget makes a distinction between appropriations for commitments and appropriations for payments.

BOX 1

Commitment and Payment appropriations

Commitment appropriations are the total cost of legal obligations which can be entered into during the current year, for activities which will lead to payments in the current and future years.

Payment appropriations are actual transfers of cash from the Community Budget to creditors during the current year, resulting from commitments made in the current or previous years.

9.   The brevity of this report reflects that it is a relatively quiet year in budgetary terms: this Financial Perspective is well established; negotiations for the next Financial Perspective have not yet commenced in earnest; and there are no extraordinary items (such as last year's decision on funding the Galileo satellite system). The Minister also explained that delayed payments from programmes agreed under the previous Financial Perspective were considerably smaller than last year; in addition some programmes under the current seven-year cycle were not yet ready to draw down payments to which they were entitled (Q 5). This is one reason why the Budget has not grown in real terms compared with the 2008 Budget, and the levels of payments expected in 2009 are lower than in 2008.

10.   In this report, we use values denominated in euro to make year-on-year comparisons. Changes in the euro-sterling exchange rate in the last year have had a significant impact upon the size of the Preliminary Draft Budget when

it is denominated in sterling.[2] As United Kingdom contributions to the EC Budget are made in sterling, the appreciation of the Euro will increase the size of the contribution. We did not question the Minister on this subject as there will always be fluctuations in exchange rates affecting the United Kingdom's contribution to, and abatement from, the budget; however the recent strength of the euro makes the increase in the United Kingdom's contribution more evident this year.[3]

11. We did however ask the Minister about the impact of inflation on the budget forecasts. We note that the Commission may use amending budgets to request additional resources following the adoption of the budget. **We shall closely scrutinise any such amending budgets should they be presented in 2009, and recommend that the Government seeks to ensure that realistic inflation forecasts are used by the Commission at this stage to prevent the need for later amendments** (p 19, QQ 9–10).

Total commitment appropriations

12. As the table on page 9 shows, the Commission's Preliminary Draft Budget envisages a total of €134.4 billion for commitment appropriations. This represents an increase of €4,086 million or 3.1% over the 2008 Budget but still leaves a margin of €2,638 million below the Financial Perspective ceiling.

Total payment appropriations

13. The table also indicates a proposed total of €116.74 billion for payment appropriations. This represents a decrease of €3,932 million, or 3.3%, against the 2008 Budget. The proposed level of payments is equivalent to 0.90% of EU Gross National Income. This is lower than the 2008 Preliminary Draft Budget, when it was 0.97% of EU GNI, and is significantly below the Own Resources Decision ceiling of 1.24%.

14. The Minister highlighted the fact that the Commission has improved its budget making process and the size of the budget surplus (unspent funds that are returned to Member States at the end of the year) has decreased by 90% since 2001 (QQ 6–7). While this reflects a generally improved alignment between the budget and outturn, the Government expressed specific concerns about programme implementation under some expenditure headings in the 2009 Budget. These are considered under the relevant heading below.

---

[2] The Government uses the exchange rate on 30 April 2008, €1 = £0.7902, in its Explanatory Memorandum. Last year's equivalent used the rate on 31 May 2007, €1 = £0.6801. This results in is a rise in sterling of 16.1%.

[3] VAT, GNI and UK abatement payments are converted from the euro figures shown in the adopted EC Budget, or any amending Budgets, using the exchange rate on the last working day of the preceding year.

TABLE 1

Summary of 2009 PDB Proposals—EUR million and GBP million

Heading		2008 Budget				2009 PDB				Change 2008 to 2009					
		Commitments		Payments		Commitments		Payments		Commitments			Payments		
		€	£	€	£	€	£	€	£	€	£	%	€	£	%
1	Sustainable growth	58,388	46,099	50,321	39,764	60,104	47,494	45,199	35,716	1,766	1,395	3.0	-5,121	-4,047	-10.2
1a	Competitiveness for growth and employment	11,082	8,757	9,769	7,719	11,690	9,327	10,285	8,127	608	480	5.5	516	408	5.3
1b	Cohesion for growth and employment	47,256	37,342	40,552	32,044	48,414	38,257	34,914	27,589	1,158	915	2.5	-5,637	-4,454	-13.9
2	Preservation and management of natural resources (CAP)	55,560	43,904	53,238	42,069	57,526	45,457	54,835	43,331	1,966	1,554	3.5	1,597	1,262	3.0
	Of which market related expenditure and direct payments	41,006	32,403	40,890	32,311	42,860	33,868	42,814	33,382	1,854	1,465	4.5	1,925	1,521	4.7
3	Citizenship, Freedom, Security and Justice	1,612	1,274	1,523	1,192	1,468	1,160	1,266	1,000	-144	-114	-9.0	-243	-192	-16.1
3a	*Freedom, security and justice*	730	577	534	422	839	663	597	472	110	87	15.0	62	49	11.7
3b	*Citizenship*	883	698	975	770	629	497	669	529	-254	-201	-28.8	-306	-242	-31.4
4	EU as a global partner	7,311	5,777	8,113	6,411	7,440	5,879	7,579	5,989	129	102	1.8	-533	-421	-6.6
5	Administration	7,282	5,754	7,282	5,754	7,648	6,043	7,648	6,043	366	289	5.0	366	289	5.0
6	Compensation	207	164	207	164	209	165	209	165	2	2	1.2	2	2	1.2
Total		130,309	102,970	120,669	95,353	134,395	106,199	116,736	92,245	4,086	3,229	3.1	-3,932	-3,107	-3.3
Margin						2,638	2,085								
Compulsory expenditure		42,530	33,607	42,472	33,561	44,532	35,189	44,514	35,175	2,002	1,582	4.7	2,042	1,614	4.8
Non-compulsory expenditure		87,779	69,363	78,196	61,760	89,863	71,010	72,222	57,070	2,084	1,647	2.4	-5,974	-4,690	-7.6
As a percentage of GNI		1.04%		0.96%		1.04%		0.90%							

Note: Due to rounding, the sum of the lines may not equal the total. Conversion rate as of 30 April 2008, €1 = £0.7902.

Margin refers to the difference between total commitment appropriations and the ceiling allowed under the Financial Perspective.

Source: HM Treasury Explanatory Memorandum (p xx)

Detail by expenditure heading

TABLE 2
Sustainable growth—EUR million and GBP million

Heading		2009 PDB				Change 2008 to 2009					
		Commitments		Payments		Commitments			Payments		
		€	£	€	£	€	£	%	€	£	%
1	**Sustainable growth**	**60,104**	**47,494**	**45,199**	**35,716**	**1,766**	**1,395**	**3.0**	-5,121	-4,047	-10.2
1a	Competitiveness for growth and employment	11,690	9,327	10,285	8,127	608	480	5.5	516	408	5.3
1b	Cohesion for growth and employment	48,414	38,257	34,914	27,589	1,158	915	2.5	-5,637	-4,454	-13.9

15. Overall expenditure in this category for commitments is €96 million under the Financial Perspective ceiling.

16. In Heading 1a (Competitiveness for Growth and Employment), the increases in commitment appropriations are largely accounted for by programmes that the Commission considers key to the implementation of the Lisbon Strategy for Jobs and Growth. These include the following:

   - 7th Research Framework Programme (increase of €631 million or 10.4%, following a rise of a similar magnitude last year);

   - Competitiveness and Innovation Programme (increase of €71 million or 17.2%);

   - Lifelong Learning Programme (increase of €60 million or 6%).

17. The increase in commitments under Heading 1b (Cohesion for Growth and Employment) is €1,158 million or 2.5%, while payments under the Heading decrease by €5,637 million or 13.9%. This is primarily due to a decrease in payments under the Structural Funds as projects agreed under the 2000–2006 Financial Perspective reach their conclusion before projects under the current Perspective are fully operational. The Minister noted that 60% of structural fund spending goes to wealthier Member States and that the Government was pushing for fundamental reform in this area (QQ 3–4). This is an issue we have discussed recently (European Union Committee, 19th Report (2007–08): *The Future of European Regional Policy* (HL 141)).

TABLE 3
Preservation and management of natural resources—EUR million and GBP million

Heading		2009 PDB				Change 2008 to 2009					
		Commitments		Payments		Commitments			Payments		
		€	£	€	£	€	£	%	€	£	%
2	**Preservation and management of natural resources (CAP)**	57,526	45,457	54,835	43,331	1,966	1,554	3.5	1,597	1,262	3.0
	Of which market related expenditure and direct payments	42,860	33,868	42,814	33,382	1,854	1,465	4.5	1,925	1,521	4.7

18. Commitment appropriations under Heading 2 (Preservation and Management of Natural Resources) rise by €1,966 million or 3.5%, and are €2,133 million under the ceiling agreed by the Financial Perspective. 74.5% of commitments under this Heading are allocated to "Market related expenditure and direct aids", which receives €1,954 million (4.8%) more than last year, and 23.3% to "Rural development", which receives €99 million more (0.7%). The Preliminary Draft Budget does not take into account the proposals made in the CAP Health Check, but if its proposals are adopted the Commission plans to incorporate these before the Draft Budget is finalised.

19. The Government recognised that the increase in direct payments had already been set by the Financial Perspective, but signalled their intent to ask the Commission to examine whether rising food prices would allow further reductions in interventions in agricultural markets (p 5). However, the Minister did not suggest that any money released should automatically be diverted to rural development, but that instead the opportunity should be taken to reform the Common Agricultural Policy fundamentally with a decision on where to channel the unused funds to be taken at a later date (QQ 23–28). This is also an issue which we have discussed recently (European Union Committee, 7th Report (2007–08): *The Future of the Common Agricultural Policy* (HL 54)).

TABLE 4

Freedom, Security, Justice and Citizenship—EUR million and GBP million

	Heading	2009 PDB				Change 2008 to 2009					
		Commitments		Payments		Commitments			Payments		
		€	£	€	£	€	£	%	€	£	%
3	**Citizenship, Freedom, Security and Justice**	1,468	1,160	1,266	1,000	-144	-114	-9.0	-243	-192	-16.1
3a	Freedom, security and justice	839	663	597	472	110	87	15.0	62	49	11.7
3b	Citizenship	629	497	669	529	-254	-201	-28.8	-306	-242	-31.4

20. Proposed commitments under Heading 3 (Freedom, Security, Justice and Citizenship) leave a margin of €55 million under the Financial Perspective ceiling. Following a substantial increase in commitments in last year's Budget, funding for "Solidarity and management of migration flows" rises by a further 16.6% (€65 million).

21. The Government expressed concerns about the size of the margin[4] under this Heading and stated that they will be looking for reductions in spending to ensure that there was sufficient reserve to meet any unforeseen future expenditure (p 5). The Minister explained that these savings might be achieved by bearing down on unrealistic implementation forecasts: last year, only 29.6% of the budgeted provision for "Solidarity and management of migration flows" was spent, and only 22.7% of funding for "Fundamental

---

[4] Margin is the difference between planned commitment appropriations and the expenditure ceilings set out in the Financial Perspective.

rights and justice" was taken up (QQ 11–14). **We support the Government's aim to ensure that the budget appropriations reflect amounts that can realistically be spent under each Heading.**

22. The decreases in payments and commitments under Heading 3b (Citizenship) are largely due to the presence of €260 million of Solidarity Fund expenditure in the 2008 Budget: due to its contingent nature, the Solidarity Fund is not allocated resources in the Budget until an application is approved.[5]

TABLE 5

The EU as a global partner—EUR million and GBP million

	Heading	2009 PDB				Change 2008 to 2009					
		Commitments		Payments		Commitments			Payments		
		€	£	€	£	€	£	%	€	£	%
4	**EU as a global partner**	**7,440**	**5,879**	**7,579**	**5,989**	129	102	1.8	-533	-421	-6.6

23. Proposed commitments under Heading 4 are €244 million under the Financial Perspective ceiling. The Commission highlights three items that may lead to this margin being used: additional activity in the Middle East (in line with the priorities of the 2009 Annual Policy Strategy); the settlement of the status of Kosovo; and the increases in prices on world food markets which may influence the EU's capacity to meet its food aid commitments. It is not clear, however, whether the margin is sufficient to meet these potential additional commitments.

24. The decrease in payment appropriations is largely due to a €700 million reduction in payments under the Instrument for Pre-accession Assistance. Notable increases of commitment appropriations are for the Development and Cooperation Instrument (by €112 million (5.0%)) and the Instrument for Stability (by €78 million (42.9%)).

TABLE 6

Administration—EUR million and GBP million

	Heading	2009 PDB				Change 2008 to 2009					
		Commitments		Payments		Commitments			Payments		
		€	£	€	£	€	£	%	€	£	%
5	**Administration**	**7,648**	**6,043**	**7,648**	**6,043**	366	289	5.0	366	289	5.0

25. The margin under Heading 5 is €129 million. The Commission explains that the 5% increase in costs is primarily driven by a 7.6% increase in pension contributions, and a request by the Commission itself for a 4.5% increase in its own budget. Within the Commission, IT costs rise by 11.9% and total staff remuneration by 6.6%. An additional 250 posts—the final tranche of the 850 new posts agreed after the accession of Romania and Bulgaria—are scheduled to be created. Over one quarter of these posts will work in the translation and language services. Other than these 250 positions, the Commission is not recruiting any additional staff. The Government indicate their commitment to ensuring that efficiency gains are being made (p 5).

---

[5] The Solidarity Fund provides aid to Member States and countries negotiating accession in the event of a major natural disaster.

26. We asked the Minister about the Government's plans to "closely scrutinise the efficiency of the EU agencies" (p 5).[6] The Minister and her officials highlighted the declaration made last summer that required the Commission to provide budgetary estimates of the staffing and surpluses of agencies, and the February Council conclusions that pushed for a review of the efficiency of the agencies (QQ 29–34). The Minister highlighted that the year-on-year increase in commitment appropriation for agencies was 1.8% (p 19). This is below the rate of growth of commitment appropriations for the budget as a whole (3.1%). **We welcome the initiatives to enhance scrutiny of the EU agencies and look forward to a review of their efficiency.**

27. The Minister explained that no decisions on Lisbon Treaty implementation would be made until ratification in all Member States has occurred. As a consequence, this Preliminary Draft Budget had not included costs for the institutional innovations introduced by the Treaty such as the new status of the High Representative for Foreign Affairs and Security Policy or the European Council President (Q 2).

28. Finally, Heading 6 of the budget provides for compensation payments to Bulgaria and Romania. These aim to improve cash-flow in their national budgets and finance control actions at the new external borders of the Union. This is the sixth and final year that these payments will be made.

The 2008/09 Budget Review

29. The European Council of December 2005 agreed that the Commission "should carry out a comprehensive reassessment of the financial framework, covering both revenue and expenditure, to sustain modernisation and to enhance it, on an ongoing basis". The Commission was asked to conduct a "full, wide ranging review covering all aspects of EU spending, including the CAP, and of resources, including the UK rebate, to report in 2008/9".[7]

30. This review began in late 2007 with the publication of a consultation paper by the Commission. Responses to the paper were initially required by mid-April, and we submitted a response before that deadline, which is published in Appendix 2. The Commission then extended its deadline to 15 June, four days after the evidence session with the Minister. The Minister emphasised that the delay was to enable more submissions to be made, rather than because the Commission had lost interest in reform (QQ 37–38).

31. We asked the Minister whether the Government planned to make a formal response to the Review. We were told that while the Government had submitted "an enormous amount of informal views", they had not yet decided whether to make a formal submission (QQ 39–43). The Government did later decide to respond to the consultation[8] and called for the re-orientation of the budget towards three areas:

   • Building a prosperous Europe within a strong global economy;

   • Addressing the challenges of climate change; and

   • Ensuring security, stability and poverty reduction.

---

[6] A number of specialised and decentralised EU agencies have been established to support the Member States and citizens. Each focuses on tasks of a legal, technical and/or scientific nature.

[7] 15915/05.

[8] HM Treasury *Global Europe: vision for a 21st century budget,* June 2008.

The Government calls for the abolition of price support and direct intervention in agricultural markets, and for other payments under the CAP to focus on delivering environmental benefits to society that would not otherwise be delivered by the market. The Government also argues that funding for the Competitiveness and Employment Objective of the EU's regional policy, currently available to all but the poorest regions in the EU, should not be available to richer Member States.

32. Further progress on the budget review is expected later this year, and we shall return to this subject when the Commission publishes its proposals for change.

Public understanding of the EC Budget

33. The Government's focus on climate change follows the Commission's emphasis on the environment in its press release about the 2009 Preliminary Draft Budget.[9] The press release indicated that 10% of funds would be spent on environmental targets and we took the opportunity to ask the Government whether enough money was allocated in the draft budget to climate change issues. The Minister said that the issue was "a very real and pressing challenge, but simply translating that into requiring a large budget line does not automatically logically follow" (Q 18). The Minister highlighted different projects under various budget Headings which were all related to climate change issues, and indicated that the Government believed climate change to be "a more valid area for EU work than the Common Agricultural Policy" (Q 20).

34. The Minister agreed that the distribution of funds for action on climate change under different Headings did not facilitate public understanding of the budget. She suggested that the different initiatives should be listed more clearly in a note to the budget that could be used to highlight the total expenditure on this subject (Q 18). **We would welcome the provision of consolidated figures for related expenditure on particular topics that are distributed across several Headings in the budget, and hope that the Government will take forward this suggestion with the Commission**.

---

[9] European Commission Press Release IP/08/695, 6 May 2008.

APPENDIX 1: SUB-COMMITTEE A (ECONOMIC AND FINANCIAL AFFAIRS, AND INTERNATIONAL TRADE)

Sub-Committee A

The members of the Sub-Committee which conducted this inquiry were:

Baroness Cohen of Pimlico (Chairman)
Lord Haskins
Lord Kerr of Kinlochard
Lord Maclennan of Rogart
Lord Moser
Lord Renton of Mount Harry
Lord Steinberg
Lord Trimble
Lord Watson of Richmond
Lord Woolmer of Leeds

Declaration of Interests

A full list of Members' interests can be found in the Register of Lords Interests:

http://www.publications.parliament.uk/pa/ld/ldreg.htm

APPENDIX 2: THE COMMITTEE RESPONSE TO THE 2008/9 EU BUDGET REVIEW CONSULTATION PAPER

1   Has the EU budget proved sufficiently responsive to changing needs?

No. The allocation of funding from the EU Budget remains dominated by historic influences. We welcome the review as an opportunity to remove many of these and start afresh with a budget which is suitable for the issues which the community currently faces.

2   How should the right balance be found between the need for stability and the need for flexibility within multi-annual financial frameworks?

We support the principle of multi-annual financial frameworks. The stability and certainty of funding that they produce is particularly welcome for regions and projects that are receiving funds from the Cohesion and Structural Funds, and similar schemes, as it allows the project managers to plan over several years rather than rush to distribute funding.

3   Do the new policy challenges set out in the consultation document effectively summarise the key issues facing Europe in the coming decades?

Yes. The list of challenges in section 2.1 of the document is comprehensive and wide-ranging. As the document implies, financial resources are just one policy lever that is available to the commission, and we would not expect the European Union budget to have to fund activities under all of these headings. National governments must take steps to address many of these factors themselves. All areas clearly need to be properly justified against the criterion of EU value added.

4   What criteria should be used to ensure that the principle of European value added is applied effectively?

The Consultation Paper summarises the case for spending from the EU budget. European action should provide clear additional benefits compared to action by individual Member States alone in pursuing policies that promote the European common interest. It is important to remember that the Commission can act as a repository of information and best practice, and co-ordinate Member States' activities, rather than directly spending money itself.

5   How should policy objectives be properly reflected in spending priorities? What changes are needed?

Direct income support under the CAP should be progressively phased out over the course of the next Financial Perspective. A significant proportion of the funds released should remain earmarked for the rural development element of the policy. There is a place for collective EU investment in ensuring that Europe has a dynamic economy—because that depends on the EU as a whole improving capacity and therefore investment in innovation and human capital. As long as the principle of subsidiarity is respected, we believe there is a place for collective EU investment in Research and Development (R&D), education and infrastructure programmes, but this investment can only reach its potential in a fully realised Internal Market.

We are currently considering the Structural & Cohesion Funds and a report will be published in May. Our preliminary conclusions are that funding should be concentrated on the new Member States, where the lack of administrative capacity is a significant impediment to growth; spending on these programmes should not occur in wealthier regions. EU cohesion spending should remain transitional, time limited and geographically focused to assist with economic convergence, restructuring or diversification. The support should be tapered and it should not become a permanent policy instrument used by the EU to prop up regions on a continuing basis.

6   *Over what time horizon should reorientations be made?*

Reorientations should be completed as soon as possible. A prompt conclusion to the Budget Review would allow the necessary groundwork to be laid for new programmes and policies before the end of this Financial Perspective.

7   *How could the effectiveness and efficiency of budget delivery be improved?*

Developments in the value for money and performance auditing side of the Court of Auditors' work would be particularly valuable. The Court already produces some special reports which go beyond simple audit function, and this is a role that could be expanded further. We also support work undertaken by Eurostat to ensure that reliable and comparable statistics are available in all countries: these are often the only means by which the success or otherwise of an intervention can be measured. It is important that this work continues and that comprehensive economic data is available for all regions of the EU.

8   *Could the transparency and accountability of the budget be further enhanced?*

The lack of a positive assurance from the European Court of Auditors in their annual Statement of Assurance is a serious problem for the European Union and the governments of its Member States. We recognise, however, that the EU budget is relatively small compared to the total government spending in many Member States and that the resolution of the failure to produce a positive assurance will require Member State commitment to change.

We encourage the Court to put in place measures clearly to distinguish between irregularity and fraud and to publish separate figures for the level of fraudulent transactions and administrative mistakes. Whilst the distinction between fraud and other irregularities must be made clear, we consider that administrative mistakes could still indicate deficiencies in the control systems operated by the Member States or the Commission. Attention should therefore be drawn to both categories and all sources of error should be taken into account when calculating material error rates.

The European Court of Auditors should produce a list of those Member States demonstrating poor management of European funds. We consider that such a list would encourage all the governments of the Member States to take this issue seriously. We consider it particularly unacceptable for the government of a Member State to treat European money with less care than national funds and urge the Council to make this clear. We are also concerned about the variability of control standards between Member States. We consider that all European expenditure should be subject to equivalent standard of control to ensure that the risk of fraud and error is minimised.

We are strongly in favour of a national Statement of Assurance on the monies disbursed in each Member State. Such a Statement should be sent to national parliaments as well as to the Commission as we consider that this will encourage the Member States to take responsibility for the systems and controls they operate. Consideration should be given to ensuring the length of time the discharge procedure takes is not extended. We do not consider that a national Statement of Assurance requires a political signature.

We recognise the commitment which the Commission has shown to improving its accounting system. This must continue and the Commission must always aim to be a global leader in public accounting.

9   Could enhanced flexibility help to maximise the return on EU spending and political responsiveness of the EU budget?

This is not necessary. The EU budget is best placed to consider wide-ranging, long-term issues where a multinational approach is most likely to effect change. It should not aim to be responsive to political pressures which vary more frequently. National government budgets can fulfil this role instead.

10   What principles should underpin the revenue side of the budget and how should these be translated in the own resources system?

In principle we would welcome greater simplicity, transparency and a reduced administrative burden. But we would not wish to propose change for change's sake. We therefore see no need for change with respect to the Traditional Own Resources. On balance we believe it would be no great loss if the VAT Resource were eliminated. We welcome Eurostat's continuing work to enhance the comparability, exhaustiveness and reliability of Gross National Income data, but we believe it already is sufficiently reliable to provide the statistical base for a revenue stream. We reject suggestions that the GNI-based revenue stream, or any other transfer from a Member State, is not a valid funding mechanism.

We do not think a tax on citizens is needed to fund the EU. Any assessment of the suitability of a tax or revenue generating measure will be subjective and dependent on the weightings placed on the different attributes considered desirable. Considered against the criterion of suitability for revenue raising (which should be the Commission's sole concern), none of the alternatives as currently set out demonstrate compelling advantages over the present system.

11   Is there any justification for maintaining correction or compensatory mechanisms?

If real reform of the expenditure side of the Budget were secured the scale of, and possibly the need for, the corrections and compensatory mechanisms would be reduced. The pressing need for reform is on the expenditure side, and in particular in the area of direct agricultural income support for farmers: without it, the case for maintaining rebate mechanisms will remain strong.

12   What should be the relationship between citizens, policy priorities, and the financing of the EU budget?

We welcome the changes to the budget that have been made by the Lisbon Treaty, in particular the removal of the principle of "compulsory" expenditure which will enhance the role of the European Parliament.

There is also a role to be played by national Parliaments. We have found it very useful to produce a report on the draft annual budget each year. Sub-committee A of the House of Lords European Union Committee meets a United Kingdom Treasury Minister between the publication of the Preliminary Draft budget and the July Budget ECOFIN meeting. The Minister is asked to outline the Government's stance on the budget and is made aware of Parliament's views.

Wider publicity could be given to the Annual Policy Strategy (APS) by the Council and national governments. The Commission must also explain clearly in the APS the financial constraints around it, and the ways in which the Commission can or cannot change its spending priorities within the financial framework. Political priorities must be matched in budgetary terms, and to do that it needs to declare which areas of action are receiving less funding in order to allow it to prioritise others. The Commission, the Council and the Parliament need to forge a closer link between the budgetary and legislative processes.

Ultimate responsibility lies in the Council, so it is crucial that it assists any effort to increase the correlation between political priorities and financial resources. The APS must provide the clear, overarching strategy for the Commission's coming year, indicating in each area what are to be the key policy intentions to be prioritised for implementation of that strategy.

As outlined in our answer to question ten, we oppose a direct tax on citizens or business.

This response draws on reports recently published by the Committee, including:

- The Future of the Common Agricultural Policy (7th Report, 2007–08; HL 54) 6 March 2008

- The 2008 EC Budget (33rd Report, 2006–07; HL 160) 30 July 2007

- Funding the European Union (12th Report, 2006–07; HL 64) 14 March 2007

- Financial Management and Fraud in the European Union: Perceptions, Facts and Proposals (50th Report, 2005–06; HL 270) 13 November 2006

- The 2007 EC Budget (39th Report, 2005–06; HL 218) 10 July 2006

- Future Financing of the European Union (6th Report, 2004–05; HL 62) 9 March 2005

These are all available online at

http://www.publications.parliament.uk/pa/ld/ldeucom.htm

The response also draws on comments made by Lord Grenfell in the House of Lords on 28 February 2008, during a debate on the report of the European Union Committee, The Commission's Annual Policy Strategy for 2008 (23rd Report, Session 2006–07, HL Paper 123).

http://www.publications.parliament.uk/pa/ld200708/ldhansrd/text/80228–0013.htm#08022878000205

The Committee plan to conduct an inquiry into the proposals for the Budget Review when they are available.

APPENDIX 3: THE ANNUAL EUROPEAN BUDGET CYCLE

Budgetary Procedure and compulsory expenditure

The budgetary procedure is set out in Article 272 of the Treaty establishing the European Community, which stipulates the sequence of stages and the time limits which must be respected by the two arms of the budgetary authority which together establish the annual budget: the Council of Ministers (acting by qualified majority) and the European Parliament.

Under the present budgetary procedure, the Council has the final say on compulsory expenditure. This is spending that is a direct result of Treaty application or of acts adopted in accordance with the Treaty. In practice this mainly means spending on agricultural guarantees. The European Parliament has the final say on all other categories of spending, which are defined as non-compulsory expenditure. Examples of non-compulsory expenditure include spending on regional policy, research policy and energy policy.

If the Lisbon Treaty is implemented, changes will be made to this procedure. Most significantly, the distinction between compulsory and non-compulsory expenditure will be abolished and the Council and Parliament will have to reach agreement on all parts of the budget. In our impact assessment of the Lisbon Treaty, we concluded that this change would increase transparency and make the agricultural budget more open and balanced between market related expenditure and funding for rural development.[10]

The Lisbon Treaty also introduces a "subsidiarity check" which allows Member State Parliaments to express concerns on subsidiarity directly to the institution which initiated the proposed legislation. Member State Parliaments working together can request a review of legislative proposals. We do not expect this procedure to apply to the budgetary process outlined below, and asked the Minister if the Government agreed. The Minister said that the Government did not have "formal legal resolution" of the issue yet, but that their initial analysis was that the subsidiarity check would apply to the making of policy rather than its implementation through the budget process (QQ 35–36).

The stages of the annual budget

In practice,[11] the stages in the negotiations over the annual budget are as follows:

(1) The Commission draws up a Preliminary Draft Budget (PDB) in May;

(2) The Council conducts its first reading of the PDB in July and establishes a Draft Budget;

(3) The European Parliament conducts its first reading in October on the basis of the Council's Draft Budget;

(4) In November, the Council conducts a second reading on the Draft Budget to consider any amendments or proposed modifications by the European Parliament; and

(5) In December the European Parliament reviews the Council's proposals and adopts the Budget.

---

10 European Union Committee, 10th Report (2007–08): *The Treaty of Lisbon: an impact assessment* (HL 62).

11 Article 272 of the Treaty establishing the European Community contains later backstop dates.

This report deals with the Preliminary Draft Budget as issued by the Commission on 6 May 2008. This version of the Budget represents the first stage of the procedure and provides the basis for subsequent negotiations between the Council and the European Parliament. Following the establishment of the Draft Budget at the 17 July Economic and Financial Affairs Council the negotiations will continue along the following lines.

The Council's Second Reading

After the Parliament's first reading, a delegation from the Parliament attends a conciliation meeting with the Council prior to the Council conducting its second reading in early November. The Draft Budget is amended in the light of the European Parliament's amendments (for non-compulsory expenditure) or proposed modifications (for compulsory expenditure). As a general rule, the Council's decisions on second reading determine the final amount of compulsory expenditure: unless the entire Budget is subsequently rejected by the European Parliament, the Council has the "last word" on this category of expenditure. The Draft Budget as amended is then returned to the European Parliament.

The European Parliament's Second Reading and the adoption of the Budget

In December the European Parliament reviews non-compulsory expenditure, for which it can accept or refuse the Council's proposals. If there is agreement, the President of the European Parliament then declares the Budget adopted and it can be implemented; alternatively the Parliament may reject the draft budget and ask for a new draft to be submitted.

Resources for the EC Budget

The revenue side for the annual EC Budget has four main sources, collectively known in the Community as the 'Own Resources'. These are:

(1) customs duties;

(2) agricultural levies, including sugar levies;

(3) a contribution based on a harmonised base for VAT income in Member States; and

(4) contributions from Member States based on a proportion of their GNI.

Under Article 269 of the Treaty establishing the European Community, the Council, acting unanimously, lays down the provisions governing the EC's Own Resources. A maximum level for Own Resources of 1.27% EU Gross National Product (GNP) was set in 1988. This has subsequently been changed to 1.24% of EU GNI. This change merely reflects the preference for using GNI as a statistical tool, and does not represent a change in the level of the ceiling.

Over time, the proportions of income from each resource have adjusted to the current position whereby the GNI-based contribution is the primary source of income for the EC Budget. In 2007, we supported this development; we found that no new form of taxation put to us provided the same level of clarity and certainty as the GNI-based resource.[12]

---

[12] European Union Committee, 12th Report (2006–07): *Funding The European Union* (HL 64).

APPENDIX 4: GLOSSARY

CAP   Common Agricultural Policy

EC   European Communities

EU   European Union

GNI   Gross National Income

GNP   Gross National Product

PDB   Preliminary Draft Budget

VAT   Value Added Tax

APPENDIX 5: REPORTS

Recent Reports from the Select Committee

Priorities of the European Union: evidence from the Minister for Europe and the Ambassador of Slovenia (11th report session 2007–2008, HL Paper 73)

The Treaty of Lisbon: an impact assessment (10th Report session 2007–08, HL Paper 62)

The Future of the Common Agricultural Policy (7th Report session 2007–08, HL Paper 54)

The Single Market: Wallflower or Dancing Partner? (5th Report session 2007–08, HL Paper 36)

Annual Report 2007 (36th Report session 2006–07, HL Paper 181)

The Commission's Annual Policy Strategy for 2008 (23rd Report session 2006–07, HL Paper 123)

Session 2007–2008 Reports prepared by Sub-Committee A

The Future of European Regional Policy (19th Report session 2007–08, HL Paper 141)

The euro (13th Report session 2007–2008, HL Paper 90)

Solvency II (6th Report session 2007–08, HL Paper 42)

Other recent Reports prepared by Sub-Committee A

The 2008 EC Budget (33rd Report session 2006–07, HL Paper 160)

Stopping the Carousel: Missing Trader Fraud in the EU (20th Report session 2006–07, HL Paper 101)

Financial Management and Fraud in the European Union: Responses to the Report (19th Report session 2006–07, HL Paper 98)

Funding the European Union (12th Report session 2006–07, HL Paper 64)

Minutes of Evidence

TAKEN BEFORE THE SELECT COMMITTEE ON THE EUROPEAN UNION (SUB-COMMITTEE A)

WEDNESDAY 11 JUNE 2008

Present	Cohen of Pimlico, B (Chairman)	Trimble, L
	Haskins, L	Watson of Richmond, L
	Moser, L	Woolmer of Leeds, L

Explanatory memorandum by HM Treasury   **SEC (2008) 514**

PRELIMINARY DRAFT BUDGET (PDB) OF THE EUROPEAN COMMUNITIES 2009

SUBJECT MATTER

Commission Proposals, the Budget Structure and the Annual Procedure

1. The Preliminary Draft Budget (PDB) sets out the Commission's proposals for European Community expenditure in 2009. it represents the first stage in the *annual budget procedure*[1] and provides the basis for subsequent negotiations between the two arms of the Budgetary Authority (the Council and the European Parliament), which will result in the adoption of the 2009 General Budget in December.

2. The context for each year's PDB is determined by the multi-annual *Financial Perspective* (FP), which sets out annual ceilings for six headings representing areas of expenditure: 1. Sustainable Growth; 2. Preservation and Management of Natural Resources; 3. Citizenship, Freedom, Security and Justice; 4. The European Union as a Global Partner; 5. Administration; and 6. Compensation (temporary compensation to ensure that the newest Member States, Bulgaria and Romania, retain a positive budgetary balance during the first years of accession).

3. The PDB is presented in *Activity-Based Budgeting* (ABB) format with budget appropriations and resources organised by activity with the amount of appropriations and staff allocated to each activity indicated. ABB seeks to tie budgetary resources to clear policy objectives, together With appropriate performance indicators and evaluation measures and as part of the 2009 PDB the Commission also publishes *Activity Statements* providing performance information for each activity. These Present specific objectives, planned outputs, and performance measures at the level of individual budget lines as well as higher-level activity areas, in line with ABB. Negotiations on the 2009 budget will be conducted on the basis of ABB documentation.

4. As in previous years, the PDB consists of a General Statement of Revenue and the draft estimates of required appropriations for the nine separate EU institutions (European Parliament, Council, Commission, Court of Justice, Court of Auditors, Economic and Social Committee, Committee of the Regions, European Ombudsman, European Data Protection Supervisor). In addition, the Commission publish a number of Working Documents alongside the PDB, including a document containing the *Activity Statements* and a document containing *Financial Statements*.

PDB 2009—Overview

5. Presenting the PDB 2009, Dalia Grybauskaité, European Commissioner for Financial Programming and Budget commented that "this is a stable, realistic budget where we have managed to shift the centre of gravity of spending firmly to long-term economic development and employment without putting other areas at rise"[2].

6. For *commitment appropriations*, the PDB proposes a total of €134,395 million (£106,198 million)[3], or 1.04% of EU Gross National Income (GNI). This represents an increase of €4,086 million (£3,228 million), or 3.1%, above 2008 levels. The margin remaining under the global *Financial Perspective* (FP) ceiling for commitments is €2,638 million (£2,085 million).

---

[1] Terms in italics are explained in the glossary (Annex 2).

[2] *Source*: European Commission, Press Release, *Budget 2009: highest spending for growth and employment* (available from: http://europa.eu.

[3] Total expenditure broken down by heading and sub-heading is shown in tables 6 & 2 in Annex 1.

7. For *payment appropriations*, the PDB proposes a total of €116,736 million (£92,245 million), 0.90% of EU GNI. This represents a decrease of €3,932 million (£3,107 million), or 3.3%, below the 2008 Budget, in which payments represented 0.96% of GNI.

8. *Compulsory expenditure* accounts for €44,532 million (£35,189 million) of the proposed commitment appropriations and €44,514 million (£35,175 million) of the proposed payment appropriations, representing respective increases of 4.7% and 4.8% above the 2008 budget.

9. *Non-Compulsory expenditure* accounts for €87,779 million (£69,363 million) of commitment and €72,222 million (£57,070 million) of payment appropriations, representing an increase of 2.4% and a decrease of 7.6% respectively, relative to 2008 levels.

10. Tables summarising the key figures of the 2008 PDB are provided in Annex 1 (in both Euros and Sterling).

PDB 2009—Detail of Proposed Expenditure by Heading

11. Overall, proposed expenditure on Heading 1 (Sustainable Growth) is €60,104 million (£47,494 million) for commitment appropriations and €45,199 million (£35,716 million) for payment appropriations, leaving a margin of €96 million (£76 million) under the FP ceiling for commitments. Heading 1 is divided into two further headings.

12. For *Heading 1a (Competitiveness for Growth and Employment)*, the PDB proposes €11,690 million (£9,237 million) for commitments and €10,285 million (£8,127 million) for payments. Compared with the 2008 Budget this represents increases of €608 million (£480 million), or 5.5%, in commitments and €516 million (£408 million), or 5.3%, in payments.

13. The change in commitment appropriation levels is largely accounted for by proposed increases for policies that the Commission considers key to achieving the Lisbon Strategy. These include:
   — Seventh Research framework programme—a €631 million (£499 million), or 10.4%, increase;
   — Competitiveness and Innovation Programme (CIP)—a €71 million (£56 million), or 17.2%, increase; and
   — Lifelong Learning Programme—a €60 million (£47 million), or 6.0%, increase.

14. The change in payment appropriations is largely accounted for by proposed increases for:
   — Seventh Research framework programme—a €518 million (£409 million), or 8.4%, increase;
   — Trans-European Networks—a €133 million (£105 million), or 18.8%, increase; and
   — Galileo—a €2m (£49 million), or 20.7% increase.

15. For *Heading 1b (Cohesion for Growth and Employment)*, the PDB proposes commitment appropriations of €48,414 million (£38,257 million) and payment appropriations of €34,914 million (£27,589 million). These represent an increase of €1,158 million (£915 million), or 2.5%, in commitments and a reduction of €5,637 million (£4,454 million), or 13.9%, relative to the 2008 Budget The proposed increase in commitments within H1b is largely due to a €1,142 million (£902 million), or 14.0% increase, in proposed expenditure devoted to the Cohesion Fund.

16. For *Heading 2 (Preservation and Management of Natural Resources)*, the PDB proposes commitments of €57,526 million (£45,457 million) and payments of €54,835 million (£43,331 million), These represent respective increases of €1,966 million (£1,554 million), or 3.5%, and £1,597 million (£1,262 million), or 3.0%, above 2008 levels. The PDB reserves a margin of €2,113 million (£1,670 million) under the FP ceiling for commitments.

17. The increases in commitments within Heading 2 are largely accounted for by increases for:
   — Market related support and direct payments in relation to Agriculture markets—a €1,954 million (£1,544 million), or 4.8%, increase—accounted for by the phasing-in of direct aids for the new member states, which is partly offset by a €570 million (£450 million), or 11%, reduction in commitments and payments for interventions in agricultural markets.
   — Rural development—a €99 million (£78 million), or 0.7%, increase;
   — Life +—a €21 million (£17 million), or 7.8%, increase—related to intensified activities in the areas of climate change and adaptation, biodiversity, environment, public health, water and waste management; and
   — European Fisheries Fund (EFF)—a €19 million (£13 million), or 3.1% increase)—in line with the relevant legal base.

18. The increases in payments within Heading 2 are largely accounted for by increases for:

— Market related support and direct payments in relation to Agriculture markets—a €1,925 million (£1,521 million), or 4.7%, increase - accounted for by the phasing-in of direct aids for the new member states;

— EFF—a €110 million (£87 million), or 24.5%, increase—attributed to low payment levels in the 2008 Budget; and

— Life+—a €61 million (£48 million), or 39.3%, increase—attributed to low payment levels in the 2008 Budget following delay in concrete measures resulting from the final adoption of the legal base in May 2007.

19. The proposed expenditure on *Heading 3 (Citizenship, Freedom, Security and Justice)* is €1,468 million (£1,160 million) for commitments and €1,266 million (£917 million) for payments. This represents a decrease in commitments of €144 million (£114 million), or –9.0%, and a decrease in payments of €243 million (£192 million) or 16.1%, relative to 2008 levels, and leaves a margin of €55 million (£44 million) under the FP ceiling for commitments. Heading 3 is divided into two further headings.

20. For *Heading 3a (Freedom, Security and Justice)*, the PDB proposes commitment appropriations of €839 million (£663 million) and payment appropriations of €597 million (£472 million). These represent an increase to commitments of €110 million (£87 million), or 15.0%, and an increase in payments of €62 million (£49 million), or 11.7%, relative to 2008 levels. This leaves a margin below the FP ceiling of €33 million (£26 million).

21. The increases in commitments and payments within Heading 3a include:

— "Solidarity and management of migration flows"—a €65 million (£34 million), or 16.6%, increase in commitments, and a €37 million (£27 million), or 11.7%, increase in payments;

— "Security and safeguarding liberties"—a €22 million (£17 million), or 31.9%, increase in commitments, and a €37 million (£14 million), or 32.6%, increase in payments.

22. For *Heading 3b (Citizenship)*, the PDB proposes commitments of €629 million (£497 million) and payments of €669 million (£529 million). These represent overall decreases of €254 million (£201 million), or –28.8%, for commitments, and €306 million (£242 million), or –31.4%, for payments, relative to 2008 levels. This leaves a margin below the ceiling for commitments of €22 million (£18 million).

23. The decrease in commitments and payments within Heading 3b is accounted for largely by the provision of €260 million (£206 million) in EU Solidarity Fund assistance (EUSF) in 2008, which due to its contingent nature, is not allocated resources in the PDB. However there are also reductions in commitments and payments for policy areas, in particular "Other actions and programmes"[4], for which the PDB proposes reductions of: €14 million (£11 million), or –50.1%, in commitments (in particular in relation to Education and Culture) and a €56 million (£44 million), or –44.3%, reduction in payments (in particular in relation to enlargement). These reductions are partially offset by increases to other areas of Heading 3b, in particular related to decentralised agencies for which increases in commitments and payments of €16 million (£13 million), or 15.8%, and €19 million (£15 million), or 18.3%, respectively are proposed.

24. For *Heading 4 (The EU as a Global Partner)*, the PDB proposes commitments of €7,440 million (£5,879 million) and payments of €7,579 million (£5,989 million). These represent an increase in commitments of €129 million (£102 million), or 1.8%, and a decrease in payments of €533 million (£421 million), or 6.6%, relative to 2008 levels and leaves a margin of €244 million (£192 million) below the FP ceiling for commitments.

25. Significant increases in commitments within Heading 4, include:

— the Development and Cooperation Instrument (DCI)—a €112 million (£88 million), or 5.0%, increase;

— EC guarantees for lending operations—a €92 million (£73 million) increase for this area of expenditure—which did not receive any allocations in 2008; and

— Instrument for Stability—a €78 million (£61 million), or 42.9%, increase.

26. The decrease in payment appropriations within heading 4 is largely accounted for through a €700 million (£553 million), or a 23.8%, reduction in payments for the Instrument for Pre-accession Assistance (IPA). The

---

[4] Includes: Transition facility for new Member States; Subsidy for Executive Agency for Education, Audiovisual; and Culture and European Year for intercultural dialogue.

reduction in payments is partially offset by increases in payments for EC guarantees for lending operations, Common and Foreign Security Policy (CFSP), and Other actions and programmes, particularly Development and relations with ACP States.

27. For *Heading 5 (Administration)*, the PDB proposes commitments and payments of €7,648 million (£6,043 million), representing an increase of €366 million (£289 million), or 5.0% in both payments and commitments, above 2008 levels. This leaves a margin for commitments of €129 million (£102 million) below the FP ceiling. Allocations for the Commission represents the largest increase, with a €152 million (£120 million), or 4.5%, increase in commitments and payments.

28. The PDB attributes staff numbers as the primary driver for increases in commitments and payments within Heading 5. The PDB requests 250 new staff posts for the Commission, in relation to the EU-2 enlargement.

29. For *Heading 6 (Compensation)*, which now only applies to Bulgaria and Romania, the PDB proposes commitments and payments of €209 million (£165 million). These represent increases of €2 million (£2 million) or 1.2%, above 2008 levels, leaving a margin for commitments of €0.89 million (£0.70 million) below the ceiling. This is the last year for which such compensations will be provided.

MINISTERIAL RESPONSIBILITY

30. Treasury Ministers are responsible for the Government's policy on the budget of the European Communities. Other Ministers have interests in those parts of the budget that are of relevance to their departments.

INTEREST OF DEVOLVED ADMINISTRATIONS

31. Policy concerning the EC Budget is a reserved matter under the UK's devolution settlements but the devolved administrations may have an interest in some aspects of EC expenditure in these areas and have been consulted in the preparation of this EM.

LEGAL AND PROCEDURAL ISSUES

Legal basis:

32. The PDB is presented under Article 272 of the EC Treaty.

European Parliament procedure:

33. The European Parliament (EP) participates fully in the budgetary process and formally adopts the budget. The EP votes by a majority of its members, or a three-fifths majority of the votes cast, depending on the circumstances, and has the final say in setting *non-compulsory expenditure*.

Voting procedure:

34. The Council votes by qualified majority and has the final say in setting the level of *compulsory expenditure*.

Impact on United Kingdom Law:

35. None

Application to Gibraltar:

36. Not applicable

Analysis of Fundamental Rights Compliance:

37. No fundamental rights issues arise with this proposal.

APPLICATION TO THE EUROPEAN ECONOMIC AREA

38. Not applicable

SUBSIDIARITY

39. The EC Budget is a matter of exclusive Community competence and the Commission's presentation of the PDB is required by the Treaty.

POLICY IMPLICATIONS

40. As a net contributor to the EC Budget it is in the UK's interests to control growth in the EC budget, whilst working to enhance efficiency in the use of EC resources. The Government will work with like-minded Member States to maintain budget discipline and subject all areas of EC spending to rigorous scrutiny. However it should be noted that much of EC expenditure (including in relation to agriculture, structural funds and multi-annual programmes) is pre-determined by previous Financial Perspective decisions, and that in the annual budget process, the final decision on much of EC expenditure is taken by the European Parliament.

41. The Government's primary aim in the upcoming negotiations will be to respect agreed and established budgetary principles. In particular, to ensure that: spending delivers genuine value for money; global appropriations for payments are based on realistic implementation forecasts (to prevent the emergence of a large budget surplus); Financial Perspective ceilings are respected, with full accordance being given to the rules governing use of the *Flexibility Instrument*; and that *Activity-Based Budgeting* is fully factored into the budgeting process. A heading-by-heading outline of the Government's initial intended approach towards the PDB follows.

42. *Heading 1 (sustainable growth)*. The Government is supportive of appropriate expenditure on growth. However it intends to scrutinise and suggest appropriate reductions to commitment and payment levels to ensure that the margin under the *financial perspective* commitment ceiling (€96 million, £76 million) is sufficient to meet any unforeseen future expenditures, and that payment levels more accurately reflect absorption capacity.

43. *Heading 2 (Preservation and Management of Natural resources)*. The Government intends to: welcome the Commission's proposed reductions in interventions in agricultural markets and to ask the Commission to consider whether or not, in light of rising food prices, further reductions might be possible. Although it is recognised that much of the increase in direct payments has already been agreed—as is the case for direct payments related to the phasing in of the new member states—the Government intends to scrutinise the remaining increases closely.

44. *Heading 3 (Citizenship, Freedom, Security and Justice)*. The Government is supportive of appropriate EC expenditure in relation to shared challenges relating to migration, health, and crime, and terrorism. However it will be looking for appropriate reductions to the commitment and payment levels proposed to ensure that the margin under the *financial perspective* commitment ceiling is sufficient to meet any unforeseen future expenditures, and that payment levels more accurately reflect absorption capacity.

45. *Heading 4 (The European Union as a Global Partner)*. The Government supports appropriate expenditure on global challenges such as international development and Common Foreign and Security Policy (CFSP). However it will encourage the Commission to ensure appropriate absorption capacity exists for payments and to make sure that the margin under the *financial perspective* ceiling is sufficient to meet requirements for possible future contingencies including any additional requirements for Kosovo, Palestine and food aid, so that these do not pose a threat to budget discipline.

46. *Heading 5 (Administration)*. The Government is in favour of enhanced efficiency and value for money from EC institutions administration expenditure. Whilst it is recognised that much of the proposed increase in this area of expenditure is related to enlargement, which potentially limits the scope for substantial reductions, the Government intends to question what efforts have been made to find efficiency gains and economies of scale. Working with other like-minded Member States, the Government will, for example, examine the level of vacancies, the redeployment of existing staff. The Government also intends to work with like-minded Member States to closely scrutinise the efficiency of the EU agencies.

47. Subject to ratification by Member State parliaments, the Lisbon Treaty, with the establishment of the new office of President of the European Council and the High Representative and External Action Service, could introduce additional resource requirements for Heading 5. The Government intends to work with like-minded Member states to assert that, wherever possible, the costs of these new institutions are met from reprioritisation.

REGULATORY IMPACT ASSESSMENT

48. Not applicable.

FINANCIAL IMPLICATIONS

49. The UK contribution to the 2009 PDB is expected to be 15.4% pre-abatement, or 10.0% post-abatement. The actual net financial cost to the UK of the 2009 EC Budget will depend not only on the size of the budget that is finally adopted, but also on the balance between different spending programmes within the budget. This determines the level of UK receipts and subsequently affects the size of the UK's abatement in the following year.

CONSULTATION

50. Not applicable.

TIMETABLE

51. Discussion of the PDB began in Council's budget committee on 8 May 2008. On 17 July the Council will establish the Draft Budget on the basis of these discussions, which will then be forwarded to the European Parliament (EP). It is expected that the Draft Budget will be debated by the EP in a plenary session in October. The EP's amendments and modifications will be considered at the Council's second reading in November. A revised Draft Budget will then be submitted to the EP for its second reading, and formal adoption of the budget is expected by mid-December.

Kitty Ussher
Economic Secretary
HM Treasury

2 June 2008

Annex 1

Table 1

SUMMARY OF 2009 PDB PROPOSALS—EUR MILLION

Heading	2008 Budget		2009 PDB		Change 2008–09		Change 2008–09 (%)	
	CA (1)	*PA (2)*	*CA (1)*	*PA (2)*	*CA (1)*	*PA (2)*	*CA (1)*	*PA (2)*
1. Sustainable Growth	58,338	50,321	60,104	45,199	1,766	−5,121	3.0%	−10.2%
1a. Competitiveness for Growth and Employment	11,082	9,769	11,690	10,285	608	516	5.5%	5.3%
1b. Cohesion for Growth and Employment	47,256	40,552	48,414	34,914	1,158	−5,637	2.5%	−13.9%
2. Preservation and Management of Natural Resources	55,560	53,238	57,526	54,835	1,966	1,597	3.5%	3.0%
Of which: Market related expenditure and direct payments	41,006	40,890	42,860	42,814	1,854	1,925	4.5%	4.7%
3. Citizenship, Freedom, Security and Justice	1,612	1,523	1,468	1,266	−144	−243	−9.0%	−1.1%
3a. Freedom, Security and Justice	730	534	839	597	110	62	15.0%	11.7%
3b. Citizenship	883	975	629	669	−254	−306	−28.8%	−31.4%
4. European Union as a Global Partner	7,311	8,113	7,440	7,579	129	−533	1.8%	−6.6%
5. Administration	7,282	7,282	7,648	7,648	366	366	5.0%	5.0%
6. Compensation	207	207	209	209	2	2	1.2%	1.2%
TOTAL (4)	130,309	120,669	134,395	116,736	4,086	−3,932	3.1%	−3.3%
Margin			2,638					
Compulsory expenditure	42,530	42,472	44,532	44,514	2,002	2,002	4.7%	4.8%
Non-compulsory expenditure	87,779	78,196	89,863	72,222	2,084	2,084	2.4%	−7.6%
Appropriations as % of GNI	0.96%	1.04%	1.04%	0.90%				

Notes:
(1) CA = commitment appropriations
(2) PA = payment appropriations
(3) Due to rounding, the sum of the lines may not equal the total

Table 2

SUMMARY OF 2009 PDB PROPOSALS—GBP MILLION

Heading	2008 Budget		2009 PDB		Change 2008–09		Change 2008–09 (%)	
	CA (1)	PA (2)	CA (1)	PA (2)	CA (1)	PA (2)	CA (1)	PA (2)
1. Sustainable Growth	46,099	39,764	47,494	35,716	1,395	−4,047	3.0%	−10.2%
1a. Competitiveness for Growth and Employment	8,757	7,719	9,237	8,127	480	408	5.5%	5.3%
1b. Cohesion for Growth and Management	37,342	32,044	38,257	27,589	915	−4,454	2.5%	−13.9%
2. Preservation and Management of Natural Resources	43,904	42,069	45,457	43,331	1,554	1,262	3.5%	3.0%
Of which: Market related expenditure and direct payments	32,403	32,311	33,868	33,832	1,465	1,521	4.5%	4.7%
3. Citizenship, Freedom, Security and Justice	1,274	6,411	1,160	1,000	−114	−192	−9.0%	−16.1%
3a. Freedom, Security and Justice	577	422	663	472	87	49	15.0%	11.7%
3b. Citizenship	698	770	497	529	−201	−242	−28.8%	−31.4%
4. European Union as a Global Partner	5,777	6,411	5,879	5,989	102	−421	1.%8	−6.6%
5. Administration	5,754	5,754	6,043	6,043	289	289	5.0%	5.0%
6. Compensation	164	164	165	165	2	2	1.2%	1.2%
TOTAL (3)	102,970	95,353	106,199	92,245	3,229	−3,107	3.1%	−3.3%
Margin			2,085					
Compulsory expenditure	33,607	33,561	35,189	35,175	1,582	1,582	4.7%	4.8%
Non-compulsory expenditure	69,363	61,790	71,010	57,070	1,647	1,647	2.4%	−7.6%
Appropriations as % of GNI	0.96%	1.04%	1.04%	0.90%				

Notes:
(1) CA = commitment appropriations
(2) PA = payment appropriations
(3) Due to rounding, the sum of the lines may not equal the total

Sterling figures converted at the exchange rate on 30 April 2008 (€1 = £0.7902)

GLOSSARY

ABATEMENT

The UK's VAT-based contributions are abated according to a formula set out in the Own Resources Decision. Broadly this is equivalent to 66% of the difference between what the UK contributes to the EC Budget and the receipts which it gets, subject to the following points:

— the abatement applies only in respect of spending within the EU. Expenditure outside the EU (mainly aid) is excluded;

— the UK's contribution is calculated as if the budget were entirely financed by VAT; and

— the abatement is deducted from the UK's VAT contribution a year in arrears.

ACTIVITY-BASED BUDGETING (ABB)

ABB was introduced in 2002 to improve decision-making by ensuring budget allocations more closely reflect pre-defined political priorities and objectives. Similar to Public Service Agreements in the UK, ABB requires the EC Budget to be based on a clear justification for intervention and an evaluation of past performance. It also requires SMART (Specific, Measurable, Achievable, Realistic and Time-bound) objectives and future performance targets that focus on delivering value for money for the EU taxpayer.

ACTIVITY STATEMENTS

The presentation of performance information for each area of activity of the European Union, providing the main elements justifying the level of resources requested by the Commission in the PDB. The statement includes details of the resources allocated to the activity, as well as associated objectives, indicators, outputs and outcomes.

THE ANNUAL BUDGET PROCEDURE

The Community's financial year runs from 1 January to 31 December. The rules governing decisions on the EC. Budget are set out in Article 272 of the EC Treaty and in the *inter-Institutional Agreement*. The timetable is as follows:

— establishment of the preliminary draft Budget by the Commission, normally in May;

— establishment of the draft Budget by the Council in late July;

— first reading by the Parliament in late October;

— second reading by the Council in mid-November; and

— second reading by the Parliament and adoption of the Budget in mid-December.

COMMITMENT AND PAYMENT APPROPRIATIONS

The budget distinguishes between appropriations for commitments and appropriations for payments, Commitment appropriations are the total cost of legal obligations that can be entered into during the current financial year, for activities that, in turn, will lead to payments in the current and future years. Payment appropriations are the amounts of money that are available to be spent during the year arising from commitments in the budget for the current or preceding years. Unused payment appropriations may, in exceptional circumstances, be carried forward into the following year.

COMPULSORY AND NON-COMPULSORY EXPENDITURE

EC expenditure is regarded as either "compulsory" or "non-compulsory". Compulsory expenditure is expenditure necessarily resulting from the Treaty or from acts adopted in accordance with the Treaty. It mainly includes agricultural guarantee expenditure, including stock depreciation. The Council has the final say in fixing its total.

The European Parliament has the final say in determining the amount and pattern of non-compulsory expenditure. The growth of this expenditure is governed by the "maximum rate of increase". Article 272(9) of the EC Treaty provides a formula for determining this rate, unless the budgetary authority agrees an alternative figure. Under the *Inter-Institutional* Agreement the Council and Parliament agree to accept maximum rates implied by the *Financial Perspective* ceilings.

FINANCIAL PERSPECTIVE

The Financial Perspective (FP) forms the framework for Community expenditure over a period of several years. The FP for 2007–13 sets expenditure ceilings for six distinct expenditure headings (Sustainable Growth, Preservation and Management of Natural Resources, Citizenship, Freedom, Security and Justice, The European Union as a Global Partner, Administration, and Compensation), as well as global ceilings for commitments and payments. The Budgetary Authority (Council and European Parliament) is bound by these ceilings in the annual budget negotiations.

FINANCIAL STATEMENT

The presentation of financial data including balance sheets, revenue and cash flow statements, or any supporting statement that is intended to communicate an entity's financial position at a point in time and its results of operations for a period then ended.

FLEXIBILITY INSTRUMENT

The Flexibility Instrument was established under paragraph 24 of the 1999 Inter-institutional Agreement, which allows for expenditure in any given budget year of up to €200 million above the FP ceilings established for one or more budget headings. Any portion of the Flexibility Instrument unused at the end of one year may be carried over for up to two subsequent years, but the Flexibility Instrument should not as a rule be used to cover the same needs two years running, The Flexibility instrument is intended for extraordinary expenditure and may only be used after all possibilities for reallocating existing appropriations have been exhausted. Both arms of the Budgetary Authority must agree to a mobilisation of the Flexibility Instrument following a proposal from the Commission.

INTER-INSTITUTIONAL AGREEMENT

The Inter-Institutional Agreement (ll.) is a politically and legally binding agreement that clarifies the EC's budgetary procedure. Under the Treaty, the Council and the European Parliament have joint responsibility for deciding the EC Budget on the basis of proposals from the Commission. The HA sets out the way in which the three institutions will exercise their responsibilities in accordance with the Treaty, and their respect for the revenue ceilings laid down in the *Own Resources Decision*.

OWN RESOURCES DECISION

The existing arrangements for financing the EC Budget are set out in the Communities' Own Resources Decision (ORD.). The current ORD. was agreed in September 2000, entered into UK law in 2001 and took effect in 2002. It sets an own resources ceiling on the amount the Communities can raise from Member States in any one year. The ceiling is currently fixed at 1.24% of EU GNI for payments and 1.31% for commitments. As the Communities are not allowed to save or borrow, revenue must equal expenditure. Budget payments are therefore limited by the amount of Own Resources that can be called up from Member States.

The ORD lays down four sources of Community revenue, or "own resources":
— Customs duties including those on agricultural products;
— Sugar levies;
— Contributions based on VAT; and
— GNI-based contributions.

Examination of Witnesses

Witnesses: Ms Kitty Ussher, a Member of the House of Commons, Economic Secretary to the Treasury, Mr Jean-Christophe Gray and Mr Paul Bunsell, H.M. Treasury, examined.

Q1 Chairman: Can I start with the usual precautions, that this session is being recorded by engineers from Westminster Sound, so it is on the record. It will be recorded to a webcast. We ask you all to use the microphones, but I am sure you were going to do that anyway. The witnesses will get a transcript of what is said during the session. Welcome, Minister. Thank you very much for coming. I know it is a busy afternoon. We are slightly depleted because our Members are downstairs trying to avert disaster on the European Treaty.
Kitty Ussher: We are very grateful.
Chairman: I do not know that the vote will be until much, much later.
Lord Watson of Richmond: It is a very emotive noun which you used!
Lord Trimble: Some of them are down there trying to achieve it!

Q2 Chairman: Some of them are down there trying to achieve it, and some of them are possibly down there trying to achieve other things! At all events, welcome, Minister. I gather you would like to introduce your people and make an opening statement. That would be great, whichever way you would like to do it.
Kitty Ussher: Thank you very much, Baroness Cohen. It is a pleasure to be here again. It is a rather odd feeling—well, quite a good feeling for me, because I do not know if you recall when I was in this chair last year I think I was three days into the job. So I feel I have come full circle and am now extremely mature and experienced, and thanks to you for helping me to feel like that. Time will tell. I have respect for the deliberations which your Committee undertakes and for your analysis and expertise in this area. I understand, just for the record, that this hearing is scheduled slightly earlier than is usual, I think because of dire constraints running up to the Budget ECOFIN on 17 July, which I hope to attend, but it is very useful, obviously, and important for me to have this, and indeed for Parliamentary scrutiny and democracy for this session to take place in advance of that. In my team with me I have Jean-Christophe Gray, who is the team leader of the Treasury's EU finances team, and Paul Bunsell, who is our policy adviser with responsibility for the EU annual budget and financial management. I wanted to perhaps set the context of this year's budget negotiations out for you and then perhaps make a few remarks as to what we, as the British Government, are hoping to achieve. This may pre-empt some of the questions which come and if I can enjoy your patience at this time, it may actually save time a little later. First of all, the Commission's proposals for the 2009 Budget will, as in every year, be heavily scrutinised and challenged by this Government where appropriate. This year's budget negotiations will also incorporate issues associated with preparing to implement the Lisbon Treaty concerning matters affecting the annual budgetary procedure and any institutional innovations introduced by the Treaty, such as the European External Action Service, but it is very important in that context to say that these are general technical level discussions in Brussels to prepare for the implementation of the Treaty. They have begun and I think it is sensible that they should do and that we should be ready to implement the Treaty if all countries have ratified, but as you have alluded to yourself, we have not actually fully ratified it yet and we have made it clear throughout and agreed with our EU partners that no final decisions on Treaty implementation can be taken until ratification across the EU is confirmed. Our focus is obviously on ratifying the Lisbon Treaty and we need to be sensitive to that on-going process, and of course in other Member States too. Ireland is holding its referendum, hopefully, tomorrow. The Government's overall and consistently stated objective for the EC Budget is to ensure that expenditure at the EU level provides value for money, is affordable, well-managed and that the Budget is fairly financed by Member States. That will continue to be our approach towards the 2009 EC Budget and for the range of other issues that will be at play in the negotiations. In line with the agreed 2007-2013 financial framework which sets budget ceilings for annual expenditure and for the budget headings, the budget's ceiling for payments for the 2009 Budget is lower than that for 2008. There are financial programming reasons for this and it will not mean that the UK will be taking any less of a rigorous approach in advocating budget discipline and seeking to contain budget growth in light of implementation forecasts and absorption capacity. So our high level priorities for the 2009 EC Budget will therefore be ensuring that total payment appropriations are set with the objective of preventing a large budget surplus arising, ensuring that the financial framework ceilings are adhered to with adequate margins under budget heading ceilings to provide for unforeseen expenditure needs. At the more detailed level, we will continue to bear down on areas of the budget where the Government questions value for money, particular, as always, agriculture and administration expenditure and to support sufficient financing of external expenditure on development and cooperation including on food aid and CFSP missions. With reference to the very sound

conclusions of your report of last year on the 2008 EC Budget and on administration expenditure in particular, I can confirm that the Government will continue to question the Commission on what efforts are being made to find efficiency savings and economies of scale in administration spending. Recent Council conclusions in relation to the discharge of the 2006 EC Budget, which called for the better financial management of EU agencies, represent an encouraging development on this front and the Government will continue to work with like-minded Member States to examine the efficiency of agencies and EU staffing levels more generally. I want to now, if I may, turn briefly to the issues associated with the Lisbon Treaty, which I mentioned earlier, which are expected to impact on the 2009 Budget negotiations, and I again make the point that we are concerned with preparatory work and that no final decisions on Treaty implementation can be taken until ratification in all Member States is confirmed. The first set of issues will involve preparations for a new annual budgetary procedure, as foreseen by the Treaty. The second set of issues will involve budgetary planning for the institutional innovations introduced by the Treaty, such as the European External Action Service (EAS), the new High Representative for Foreign Affairs and Security Policy and the new European Council President. The Commission has agreed with the Council that presentation of the provisional budgetary allocations for these should be deferred to the autumn. It will be our aim to keep the associated costs to a minimum and to press for any additional resource requirements to be found from re-prioritisation within the Administration Budget heading. In the context, if I might add, of the wider 2008/9 Budget Review, the UK has clear priorities, as set out in the 2007 Global Europe pamphlet. They are far-reaching reform of the CAP, a significant increase in the percentage of structural and cohesion funds spent on poorer Member States and a reorientation of the Budget towards the challenges of globalisation, including promoting R&D and innovation, international development and addressing climate change. Our approach for the 2008/9 Budget Review is guided by three principles, that the EU should act where there are clear additional benefits, but where EU level action is appropriate it should be proportionate and flexible and that there should be the highest levels of financial management and administration. I was very glad, my Lord Chairman, that your Committee gave its endorsement of these principles and I can assure you I will continue to make the case for our Budget discipline priorities and these principles when I meet my Budget ECOFIN colleagues in July. Thank you for your patience in letting me make these opening remarks and I look forward to the conversations which follow.

Q3 *Chairman:* Thank you very much, Minister. Do you broadly consider that the proposals before us represent value for money?
Kitty Ussher: No, in that we think there is more that can be done. We think there is value for money in some key areas. Examples are traditional British priorities, heading 1a, for example, the Seventh Research Framework programme. We think this is useful in improving research and development activity across the EU. We think heading 1b is helpful to the extent that it facilitates economic development of less wealthy Member States. Parts of heading 3a (Freedom, Security and Justice) play a worthwhile role in complementing national efforts to combat international terrorism and manage migration flows and to share best practice in combating crime. We have traditionally supported heading 4, where spending helps to meet millennium development goals, but we think—you would expect me to say this, and it remains the case—that value for money in other areas remains questionable. We think the Common Agricultural Policy, particularly in the context, perhaps, of high food prices, is something which needs fundamental reform and we will continue to push that. We also feel that it is not a good use of European taxpayers' money that 60% of the structural fund spending goes to wealthier Member States and these are points which we will continue to push.

Q4 *Chairman:* You will perhaps know that we are currently concluding a report on the future of structural funds and there is some discussion within the Committee as to the extent to which the British Government and some of the richer states would in effect be prepared to give up substantial sums of money, we are speaking about up to £1 billion per year for the United Kingdom, to get that money to the poorer states in the EU. That was the discussion we were attempting to resolve immediately before you arrived. We have not resolved it, but I would be interested indeed, Minister, whether you think that not only us but the other net contributory wealthy states would indeed be prepared to give up really quite a lot of net receipts in order that the poorer states might benefit.
Kitty Ussher: I am afraid I cannot immediately solve the problem you were addressing a few minutes ago but, as I said this time last year, we feel we need to take a principled point here and that richer Member States have ways of addressing some of these fundamental economic disparities which are perhaps not available to poorer Member States and it is the responsibility of richer Member States to take that broader principled view. So we will be pushing in this area for fundamental reform, and indeed the British Government said as much a number of years ago, in 2003, when we set out our negotiating priorities. That

was at an earlier stage in the relevant negotiations, but it set out what our view was. I will be extremely interested to read the conclusions of your forthcoming report.

Chairman: Thank you, Minister. I am not sure if that was helpful, but it was kindly meant.

Q5 *Lord Watson of Richmond:* Given, Minister, your initial answer to the first question, do the Budget proposals represent value for money, which was a monosyllabic "No," could I ask you, therefore, whether you are actually content with the total levels of expenditure proposed by the Commission. They do not differ substantially from last year, but are you content with the total levels? You may think they are being spent on the wrong things, but are you content with the total levels?

Kitty Ussher: The total levels were set out in the seven year financial perspective. The way to look at this is that it is not simply an issue of what is the total amount being spent but what is the value for money of the underlying purpose of the expenditure, so it needs to be taken in the round. I guess there is an aspect of what is before us that it is important to recognise that the overall level has actually come down, and in that sense, in that we want to create a prioritisation, it could be seen at a headline level to be encouraging, but I think, as I said in my opening remarks, that is actually a function of the way programmes are managed over several years and what we are seeing is the beginning of the uptake of the new programmes from this financial perspective when the delays in the programmes from the previous one have reached their natural conclusions. You understand my point. So in that we want to bear down on unnecessary expenditure, the headline answer would be, yes, we are glad that the Budget is less this year, but that does not necessarily mean to say that we should not be focusing far more on making sure that it is value for money. So I would say it is not the overall level, it is how it is spent that is important. As I said in my answer to my Lord Chairman's first question, we think there are some areas where it can be spent more effectively.

Q6 *Lord Watson of Richmond:* Can I just ask one supplementary to that? However, in terms of how this Budget is perceived, particularly by public opinion, albeit the levels have slightly come down, if we ended up with one of the things you have stated as something we should avoid, namely a large surplus, would that raise fundamental questions about the totality of the Budget at the end? Do you think at this level a large surplus is a likely outcome?

Kitty Ussher: I do not think a surplus as large as some of the ones we have seen in previous years is likely, and I think that is a good thing. The important point here is that we want budget ceilings to be real, we

want there to be proper financial management and control and clear prioritisation. So obviously a little bit of a surplus is good in that it gives you a margin and some headroom for unforeseen events, but if you have a situation where you are routinely having large surpluses –

Q7 *Lord Watson of Richmond:* Then it raises fundamental questions.

Kitty Ussher: Yes, something has gone wrong in the budgeting planning process. I think we had €15 billion in 2001 and last year it was €1.5 billion, so that is a clear improvement. I think it is an indicator that someone has got their sums right if the surplus is not enormous.

Q8 *Lord Watson of Richmond:* Whereas in 2001 they definitely got them wrong?

Kitty Ussher: I think that is extremely clear, yes.

Q9 *Lord Moser:* These budgets, of course, are framed in today's prices, which is inevitable, and by comparison with last year's the Budget is not very different from last year. What interests me is that for the first time for some years Europe—not least Europe, the world, but Europe too—is facing fantastic economic uncertainties, not least in inflationary terms. I remember from my days in Whitehall we tried to get cleverer at forecasting the sensitivity of budgets depending on what happens to economies, not least inflation, so I take all these budgets with a very great pinch of salt now, not least because of the inflationary uncertainty. I am just interested in whether any work has been done by the Treasury or anywhere, or in Brussels, to add some margins of error to what is before us.

Kitty Ussher: Yes. It is not our view that the recent increases in oil and food prices, for example, throw the budgets out of kilter. There may be policy implications from those economic developments. Perhaps I can just defer to Jean-Christophe?

Mr Gray: One example is the impact of high food prices. As a result of higher food prices, there may be less requirement for market intervention through the Common Agricultural Policy. So it is possible that throughout the course of 2009 there is some surplus in that area. One of the things we will be taking into account when we are challenging the assumptions in here under heading 2 is that very issue. So I would give that as one example where there may be some consequences.

Q10 *Lord Moser:* I do not want to go on about this, but in one sense every single line in these budgets is vulnerable. Every single expenditure is vulnerable to changes. What is different between now and a year ago is that we really face some very likely major changes, especially in pricing in inflation, so I am rather surprised to hear you say that it is unlikely to affect it very much, whatever happens to European inflation.

Kitty Ussher: Obviously, the Commission has economists and macroeconomic forecasting takes place within the Commission, obviously, and will be used to inform their own budget projections. I am not sure, to be honest, if the precise mechanisms have taken that into account. I am also not sure that inflation levels are so high as to throw it out of kilter completely, but perhaps, my Lord Chairman, we can provide a note on that point to reassure you.

Lord Moser: Thank you.

Q11 *Lord Trimble:* Before I come to the substance of this, may I just interject? Speaking purely personally, I am delighted by the principled stance the Government is taking on regional policy. I hope the Committee will be able to do something to support that. However, I notice in paragraph 41 of your paper you say, "The Government's primary aim in the upcoming negotiations will be to respect agreed and established budgetary principles," and in particular you refer to global appropriations being based on "realistic implementation forecasts". That is partly, of course, to avoid surpluses. Do you think the Commission is still making unrealistic forecasts?

Kitty Ussher: I think they are better than they were, but I think we should be ever vigilant. I also think that the scrutiny and questioning which the British Government has historically provided has been shown to have had a positive effect.

Q12 *Lord Trimble:* Can you give us some examples of the unrealistic implementation forecasts which you think are still in the process?

Kitty Ussher: I am sure I can. Under heading 3a (Freedom, Security and Justice) is Solidarity and Management of Migration Flows. It looks like the implementation rate is around 30%, which obviously proves they do not get their forecasts right, and other parts of heading 3 as well, Fundamental Rights and Justice, at around 22%.

Q13 *Lord Trimble:* Expenditure compared with the forecasts were 22% and 30%?

Kitty Ussher: I will defer to the expert.

Mr Bunsell: Heading 3a is an area of poor implementation. Last year, just to give you an example of that, the solidarity and management of migration flows had an implementation rate of 29.6% and fundamental rights and justice had an implementation rate of 22.7%. In fact overall the implementation over that specific sub-heading was in the area of about 42% and yet we are still seeing increases suggested in this area for 2009. So this is an area we will be scrutinising very closely.

Q14 *Lord Trimble:* That is a remarkably low implementation rate, is it not?

Mr Bunsell: Yes, it is remarkably low. It is the lowest across the budget.

Kitty Ussher: We will be using these figures to make our points very strongly.

Lord Trimble: Thank you.

Q15 *Lord Moser:* I do not make a habit of these supplementary questions, but one more if I may on this subject of scrutiny, and so on. There is a reference somewhere, Minister, but I cannot find it now, that the task at this end lies with the Treasury, which must be right, for scrutiny of the Budget, but presumably individual Whitehall departments do their bit? The reason I ask is because I amuse myself (if that is the right term) by going through these things to see what has happened to decisions I was part of, or discussions I was part of when I was on another European Union Sub-Committee, the Social Affairs Sub-Committee. I looked up, for example, what happened to the very precise point which we spent weeks discussing, the proposal for the European Institute of Innovation and Technology which Brussels started with. We were rather against it on our Sub-Committee. This is paragraph 3.1.5. Colleagues from Whitehall, the Education Ministry, whatever it is now called, also had a great interest in it. It comes up here at €5.8 million. It is not a big sum, but has somebody actually gone through all these detailed figures, whatever is discussed in committees, and so on? Is every detailed figure in here like that one? Do you see my question?

Kitty Ussher: Not entirely.

Q16 *Lord Moser:* My question is, our fellow European Sub-Committees seem to agree with the Department of Education (as I think it was called) that this was a bad project. It ends up here with only €5.8million. I am interested in the scrutiny process, that is all.

Kitty Ussher: The process requires an enormous amount of coordination—not the scrutiny process but the actual executive decision-making process obviously requires an enormous amount of coordination and I am regularly talking to my counterparts in departments to work out what our priorities should be. In terms of the scrutiny of this Committee, I think it is extremely effective and certainly my experience as a Minister is that your report and some of the transcripts of the evidence hearings do have a huge impact on the way the Whitehall machinery (if I can crudely characterise it as such) approaches such questions. On the EIT, we do still have some concerns as to how it was proposed and implemented. We had quite a lot of success in actually renegotiating parts of the package, which meant that when it was finally presented we thought it was, on balance, a good thing and financed in just about an acceptable way, and that was the result of a lot of hard work.

Q17 *Lord Moser:* I do not want to waste your time. It is more the process point.

Kitty Ussher: Yes. As a Minister, I feel that the process is real and holds us to account and makes us portray and question our own priorities in an extremely effective way and I am grateful to you for posing the question.

Q18 *Lord Woolmer of Leeds:* Good afternoon, Minister. On page 29 of the Preliminary Draft Budget the Commission say that "climate change is expected to remain at the top of the policy agenda" in the European Union, not just reducing greenhouse emissions but also "adaptation to the negative effects of climate change" and I would like to really follow one or two things through from that. Clearly, the European Union has an important role to play in regulatory frameworks but here we are largely talking about more explicit expenditures on positive projects, and so on. My broad question is whether you feel, given the scale and urgency of climate change issues, the expenditure programmes at the European level are satisfactory in scale and urgency in addressing the various issues?

Kitty Ussher: I think it is a very real and pressing challenge, but simply translating that into requiring a large budget line does not automatically logically follow. There is a lot of scope for individual Member Governments. There is also, particularly, a scope for EU action in this area. That does not necessarily mean that that needs to be an enormous amount of spending. As an example, I think Europe is leading the world in carbon trading through the Emissions Trading Scheme and yet there is not an enormous direct spend attached to that project. But it is clearly an area where we need to work internationally and whilst there are domestic initiatives in this area, they cannot solve the problems by themselves. Another thing I am quite keen to say on the record around the EU Budget proposals for climate change is that we feel the Commission can do more to consolidate the various different relevant projects in this area. It is almost that different initiatives are scattered throughout the EU budgets and perhaps if they are brought together in some consolidated way, either as part of the normal Budget or in some kind of note form, it might be easier to see how much of the EU Budget was being spent in this area, which one would presume would lead to a higher number than is currently available.

Q19 *Lord Woolmer of Leeds:* I do not want to disagree with you, but something being important does not mean to say huge sums have to be spent on

it, but nevertheless some money has to be spent on it. Has the Government formed an estimate of how much of the Commission's proposed total spend is on climate change related issues, given the great importance our own Government appears to give to these matters?

Kitty Ussher: It is quite hard, actually, to come up with a precise number on climate change, precisely for the reason I mentioned, in terms of what the EU Budget is spent on. That is why we encourage greater transparency in this area. But it is clear where it sits, under heading 1a under the framework programme. Obviously, there is a large amount of R&D work going into climate change initiatives. Heading 2 funds adaptation projects to reduce greenhouse gas emissions, to develop green technologies and work for the development of necessary IT structures to support things like the European Emissions Trading Scheme, as I have just mentioned. Heading 4, obviously, under sustainable management of the environment, has got a number of relevant initiatives. It is probably worth making the general point that because we think the Common Agricultural Policy needs dramatic reform, we would like to see a smaller proportion of the EU Budget going on that and a larger proportion going on genuine issues which require cross-border collaboration such as climate change.

Q20 *Lord Woolmer of Leeds:* It is very helpful for you to draw our attention to the headings, of which I have spotted two, but what is the figure? You said that more should be and less on CAP. What is the balance? Give the public an idea. Is the ratio 50:1? Climate change is supposed to be an enormously important problem.

Kitty Ussher: What I said was that I thought the proportion spent on climate change—I am sorry, I am not going to be able to answer your question precisely, but the general point is that we think climate change is a more valid area for EU work than the Common Agricultural Policy.

Q21 *Lord Woolmer of Leeds:* There is one specific area of spend which our own Government is going into with a very small, modest trial scheme, and that is carbon capture and storage. A large number of European countries depend heavily on coal, including ourselves, and we are going to for the foreseeable future, and it is an area which every government, including our own, have talked about this for years and nothing has yet happened. Do you think that at the European level the budget allocated to carbon capture storage project work addresses the urgency which is needed in the area of coal-fired electricity generation?

Kitty Ussher: I completely agree with you that this is an issue which we need to explore, and I know that a commitment to that effect has been made in the last Energy White Paper of this Government. There is an amount in the EU Budget under heading 1a on carbon capture and storage research. It is a good example of where, by working together, we can pool our resources to make the necessary technological advance to make this possible. We support greater budgets being allocated to carbon capture and storage under the Framework programme.

Q22 *Lord Woolmer of Leeds:* You would?
Kitty Ussher: We would.

Q23 *Lord Haskins:* Broadly speaking, this Budget, the structure of it, was determined really by the Fichler reforms of CAP four or five years ago and the structure of it was largely going to follow that right through into 2013. However, one factor has come in which is the huge change in agricultural markets over the last couple of years, which has very much changed a lot of the assumptions behind the Budget. In other words, a lot of the subsidies are no longer triggered, they are no longer relevant, a lot of the import tariffs are no longer appropriate, and there is a short-term situation here. I know this has been reflected to an extent in the Budget, that they have taken it into account, but I suspect they have not taken it enough into account and that there is going to be more money available than people expected. However, what concerns me is that the rural community always thinks that if it does not go to farmers it goes to somebody else and it should stay within the ambience of the rural society. That is very much what is being pressed here. Do you think that the modulation process should be accelerated, that if money is saved on funding farmers that money should automatically go into rural development, or might it be more sensibly used in the other direction?
Kitty Ussher: We prefer rural development than, obviously, direct payments, so I think the realpolitik of this is important and we would support a shift from Pillar One to Pillar Two in that regard. But fundamentally we think the whole Common Agricultural Policy needs to be looked at from more of a blank piece of paper, and this is what we will be pursuing in the 2008/9 Budget Review which is just gearing up.

Q24 *Lord Haskins:* So any money, therefore, which is going to be saved from Pillar One because of the fact the markets have changed, you would say would automatically flow into Pillar Two?
Kitty Ussher: No, I am not being that specific. I am saying that as a general point if it is a choice between Pillar One and Pillar Two, we would always support modulation through to Pillar Two, but we are not

aware of a formal proposal to do something in terms of food aid or having a direct response to the rising food prices. I am very happy to talk to colleagues if and when that is put forward, but if you will permit me, I do not want to tie myself down to a definite answer on what will be in the negotiation process. I think our principles have been well laid out in terms of our attitude to the Common Agricultural Policy and is well-known to our European partners.

Q25 *Lord Haskins:* So in a way governments consistently have been sceptical about this CAP almost to the point that other people get bored by it. This is the best opportunity for looking at CAP reform that there has ever been and there must be fertile ground for constructive thinking about it?
Kitty Ussher: I could not agree more, actually, and I think there is a general point to be made that we want capacity in global food markets to rise and so to have distorting payments and subsidies in the EU system acts against the proper functioning of the food market and equating supply and demand in a way that can bring prices down in the long run. So I feel that rather than saying, "Where should this money be spent?" which we can have a debate about later on, the important thing is to use this opportunity to really ram home the arguments which people may be bored with but which are very valid from our point of view, that we need fundamental reform of the Common Agricultural Policy, because only then can we find a system where supply and demand can more easily be equated without prices having to rise to the extent which they are.

Q26 *Lord Haskins:* This, of course, relates to the WTO negotiations?
Kitty Ussher: Of course.

Q27 *Lord Haskins:* And it relates to the Irish referendum, which I gather is going to be lost because Mr Mandelson is going to get the farmers to vote "No" because of the farmers' attitude towards Mr Mandelson's views of WTO reform?
Kitty Ussher: I think it strengthens the general comment, the pragmatic, moral case.

Q28 *Lord Haskins:* As long as the British Government deals with the issue in a non-patronising way so that we actually have a sensible discussion, rather than find ourselves out on our own making rhetorical statements at a time when there is good evidence for people right across the EU accepting the need for reform.
Kitty Ussher: I will pass that on.
Mr Gray: Could I just add very briefly, on the specifics of modulation you will probably be aware that in agriculture councils under the French presidency the Common Agricultural Policy

healthcheck will be discussed and one of the proposals there is to increase compulsory modulation rates within that. More widely, as the Minister mentioned at the start, the Common Agricultural Policy and the importance of reform is an extremely important part of the debate on the Budget review which has just started in the last year or so in Europe.

Q29 *Chairman:* In your Explanatory Memorandum, you note that you work with like-minded Member States to scrutinise closely the efficiency of the EU agencies. When we discussed this briefly during the last oral evidence session we could not really think of many like-minded states. Who are our natural allies in this?

Kitty Ussher: I am delighted to be able to report that we found quite a few in the end and were able to agree cuts to allocations for agencies in the context of the 2008 Budget negotiations. I was sitting around the table at Budget ECOFIN at the end of November last year and there was actually an encouraging consensus on the need to bear down on agency costs as part of that. It was the net contributors you would expect to be particularly vocal in their support— Sweden, the Netherlands, Austria, France and Germany in particular.

Q30 *Chairman:* One must hope that they will all still be there this time.

Kitty Ussher: I would hope so, yes.

Q31 *Chairman:* Have you made any progress on agency costs?

Kitty Ussher: Yes, we have. As I have just said, we did quite substantially in the context of the 2008 Budget negotiations. I think I am right in saying also in the context of the discharge of the 2006 Budget-

Mr Gray: Yes. Paul, I think, is the expert on this one.

Kitty Ussher: It was also mentioned in the conclusions.

Mr Bunsell: Two things which were achieved were, firstly, that last July a joint declaration was agreed between Parliament and the Council requesting the Commission to provide budgetary estimates on the staffing and the surpluses of agencies along with its PDB figures for those agencies, and that enabled greater scrutiny of agencies, and indeed we have seen the growth of agency budgets slow down, possibly as a result. Secondly, quite rightly, as the Minister says, in February Council conclusions on discharge we agreed language which pushed for a review of the efficiency of these agencies.

Kitty Ussher: Great progress. It is possible.

Q32 *Chairman:* But not yet cost-cutting?

Kitty Ussher: We did get some specific costs cut in the current budget that we negotiated last year.

Q33 *Lord Woolmer of Leeds:* In the draft of the Budget for 2009 how do the figures for agencies compare with last year's?

Kitty Ussher: I am not sure I have the exact figure, but Paul does.

Mr Bunsell: I do not have specific figures, but in terms of commitment appropriations they are pretty much stagnant. In terms of payment appropriations, they have decreased.

Kitty Ussher: We will continue to bear down. We are emboldened by our success so far and believe there is scope for further –

Q34 *Chairman:* If you could write to us with the exact number, if it is not available now?

Kitty Ussher: Yes, we will write.

Chairman: Thank you very much.

Lord Watson of Richmond: I have a question about the impact of the Lisbon Treaty, although Lord Haskins has just explained to us that it will fall because of Mr Mandelson's intervention in the Irish debate tomorrow.

Lord Trimble: I think the French Parliament has just said there is likely to be more power.

Q35 *Lord Watson of Richmond:* More power! Time will tell. Not very much time will tell! As you are aware, some Members of the European Parliament Committee on Budgets have pointed to a confusion really around whether the annual budgetary cycle will in fact be subject to national Parliaments' subsidiarity check procedure which is being introduced by the Lisbon Treaty. It would be interesting to know what the Government's view is on this.

Kitty Ussher: We do not have formal legal resolution of it at the moment. However, I would say that it looks as if it is all right, we think, the reason being that the Budget is, of course, the process rather than the specific spending and we think that the intention behind the new subsidiarity process concerns the actual spending lines, the actual policies as opposed to the Budget process.

Q36 *Lord Watson of Richmond:* Yes, but your reading of Lisbon is that the subsidiarity test would be applicable?

Kitty Ussher: To the Budget, no. I cannot give you 100%, but it looks as if it is not.

Q37 *Lord Woolmer of Leeds:* The timetable for the 2008/9 Budget Review has been extended by the Commission. Do you think the Budget Review is still a priority for the Commission?

Kitty Ussher: Yes, I do. All the indications that we have at working group and indeed at Ministerial and Commissioner level are that it is extremely valid. We think the reason the timetable was extended actually makes the converse point, that it is an indication of the amount of interest there is out there and they wanted to make sure that they were consulting properly. So without prejudice to the results of it, we think that people are committed to it.

Q38 *Lord Woolmer of Leeds:* So the Commission will have received a lot of feedback in the Review, will they?
Kitty Ussher: What they say is that the amount of interest triggered across Europe is such that they wanted all interested parties to be able to contribute and have their views, so they therefore extended the deadline.

Q39 *Lord Woolmer of Leeds:* I should know, and I apologise for the fact that I have forgotten, if I did know, has HM Government submitted any views on this?
Kitty Ussher: An enormous amount of informal views. We have not submitted a specific publication at this point. We are just working out the best way to respond.

Q40 *Lord Woolmer of Leeds:* What timescale do you anticipate for when that might be forthcoming?
Kitty Ussher: Extremely soon we will be deciding how best to respond. That is the only answer I can give you at the moment. Obviously, before that decision is made, I cannot give you the answer.

Q41 *Lord Woolmer of Leeds:* So the Commission had a lot of views expressed to it, some informally by us but not yet formally by us?
Kitty Ussher: Extremely strong informal views, but no actual document published at this point. The decision is pending urgently.

Q42 *Chairman:* But you know there is a time limit?
Kitty Ussher: I am happy to let you know as soon as we decide.

Q43 *Chairman:* It has got to be before the recess, has it not?
Kitty Ussher: One would have thought so, yes, depending on the form that it takes. You will certainly hear from us before the recess.

Q44 *Lord Trimble:* I understand that the current Commission has set itself a target of a positive statement of assurance on the Budget by the end of its time in office. Do you think they are going to achieve that?
Kitty Ussher: That is a matter for them. I certainly hope that they do, yes.
Lord Watson of Richmond: It will be a first!

Q45 *Lord Trimble:* More specifically then, what progress has been made towards the publication of an audit of funds managed by the UK?
Kitty Ussher: This is our own process. Yes, as you know, we voluntarily decided to have a consolidated statement of EU funds spent in the UK and to have that audited by the NAO. There has been a slight slippage of that, but that is simply due to the fact that the NAO is undertaking a complex task for the first time, but we do expect that to be published very soon.

Q46 *Lord Trimble:* Do you think any other Member countries will follow our example?
Kitty Ussher: We always aim to lead in Europe, so I hope so. We have achieved shifting the centre of gravity on this issue. I do not have specific initiatives in other Member States.
Mr Gray: The Netherlands and Denmark have already produced these in previous years. A number of other Member States are very interested in doing so and there are a few others who are less –

Q47 *Lord Trimble:* This is going to produce an interesting situation. If the hitherto like-minded states, the states we mentioned earlier, all do this, then this is going to leave certain other countries looking quite exposed if they do not follow suit?
Kitty Ussher: That is precisely the point!

Q48 *Chairman:* Are the Irish going to attempt to follow our lead in this matter?
Mr Gray: Not that I know of.
Kitty Ussher: Unless Lord Haskins knows differently!
Lord Watson of Richmond: There is a biblical text which suggests itself about there being more rejoicing in Heaven!

Q49 *Chairman:* It remains for us to thank you, Minister, very much for coming and being so helpful in your replies, and indeed to thank all your Treasury colleagues for their help. I hope we have not unduly delayed you.
Kitty Ussher: I hope we have not unduly delayed you as well. Thank you very much. It is a pleasure. I will follow up in writing on those points.

Supplementary letter from HM Treasury

2009 PRELIMINARY DRAFT BUDGET (PDB) OF THE EUROPEAN COMMUNITIES

During the evidence session before Sub-Committee A on 11 June I agreed to write to provide further information on two issues: how inflation is incorporated into the PDB; and amount, in appropriations, requested for decentralised agencies in the 2009 PDB compared to the 2008 PDB. I will now respond to these issues in turn:

INFLATION RATES

Inflation is incorporated into the PDB through: a 2% annual inflation rate factored into the ceilings for commitments set by the financial framework; and the inclusion of inflation rates in the budgetary requirements for the year presented by the Commission and other EU institutions in the PDB. Inflation rates play an intrinsic part in determining administration costs, including staff remunerations and pensions of officials and other servants of the European Communities.

If additional information on inflation comes to light during the course of Budget negotiations that has an impact on the estimates presented in the PDB, the Commission is permitted to modify its estimates accordingly through an amending letter that needs to be presented to the Council ahead of the European Parliament's first reading in the autumn. Following the final adoption of the EC Budget, the Commission may present the Budgetary Authority with a request for additional resources in the form of an amending budget should additional unforeseen inflationary pressures occur.

DECENTRALISED AGENCIES

Compared to the 2008 PDB, the 2009 PDB sees total increases in appropriations for decentralised agencies of: €38.9 million (£31.6 million) or 7.6% in commitments, to €563.9 million (£446.8 million[1]); and €44.1 million (£34.9 million) or 8.4% increase in payments, to €571.5 million (£452.9 million). This represents an increase of €9.8 million (£7.7 million) or 1.8% in commitments and a decrease of €6.0 million (£4.8 million) or −1.0% in payments, compared to the 2008 Adopted Budget.

A detailed comparison of appropriations for decentralised agencies, by Budget Heading, requested in the 2009 PDB, 2008 PDB, are provided for in the 2008 Budget. Further details of the budgets for the decentralised agencies is contained in the Commission's Working Document Part IV, which has been placed in the library of the House for your information.

I am copying this letter to Lord Moser and Lord Woolmer, and Michael Connarty MP, Chairman of the Commons Committee.

8 July 2008

---

[1] This and all further sterling figures are converted using the exchange rate for 30 June 2008, £1 = €1.2622.

Printed in the United Kingdom by The Stationery Office Limited
7/2008   402715   19585

ISBN 978-0-10-401327-4